Pros and Cons:
Animal Testing

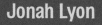

Jonah Lyon

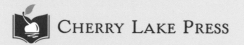

CHERRY LAKE PRESS

Published in the United States of America by Cherry Lake Publishing Group
Ann Arbor, Michigan
www.cherrylakepublishing.com

Reading Adviser: Beth Walker Gambro, MS, Ed., Reading Consultant, Yorkville, IL
Content Adviser: Silvia Alexandria Mansoor, Michigan State University College of Law, JD

Photo Credits: © Emilia Stasiak/Shutterstock, cover, 1; © wavebreakmedia/Shutterstock, 5; © simona pilolla 2/
Shutterstock, 6; © Erik Lam/Shutterstock, 7, back cover; Public Domain/Wikimedia/Uploaded by Rswarbrick, 8;
© Oleg Senkov/Shutterstock, 9; © Rido/Shutterstock, 10; © Ragne Kabanova/Shutterstock, 13; © ussr/Shutterstock, 14;
© Pressmaster/Shutterstock, 15; © glebchik/Shutterstock, 16; © Kostiantyn Voitenko/Shutterstock, 17; © Elnur/
Shutterstock, 18; © Shyntartanya/Shutterstock, 19; © sommthink/Shutterstock, 20; © AndriiKoval/Shutterstock, 21;
© Wei Ming/Shutterstock, 23; © Nelson Antoine/Shutterstock, 24; © unoL/Shutterstock, 25; © viki2win/Shutterstock, 26;
© Brian Ongoro/Shutterstock, 28; © nexusby/Shutterstock, 29; © Bricolage/Shutterstock, 30

Library of Congress Cataloging-in-Publication Data has been filed and is available at catalog.loc.gov

Cherry Lake Publishing Group would like to acknowledge the work of the Partnership for 21st Century Learning,
a Network of Battelle for Kids. Please visit *http://www.battelleforkids.org/networks/p21* for more information.

Printed in the United States of America

Jonah Lyon is an elementary school teacher who is passionate about critical thinking and honest dialogue. He believes that giving his students the tools to teach themselves about topics and think for themselves best equips them for life. In his free time, he loves to write music, exercise outside, and do charity work.

CONTENTS

Introduction

Have you ever heard the saying, "There are two sides to every story"? This means that there is always someone with a different opinion or point of view. There is always an **opposition** to a belief or claim. For instance, you might strongly be opposed to wearing socks to bed at night. But your friend thinks that's the best way to stay warm when asleep.

Many people have different opinions about what is right and wrong. But the more informed you are about the other side, the more able you are to argue for your position. Instead of telling your friend that their belief is wrong, ask them why they think wearing socks to bed is a good idea.

What is something you and your friends or family disagree about? How do you resolve the disagreement?

Sometimes facts are relevant to use as reasoning when forming a position. Other times, personal preferences—such as wearing socks to bed because you don't want your feet to get cold—are more applicable.

The more informed you are about the opposing viewpoint, the more informed your own arguments can be. This is called having a **rational discourse**.

People also use **critical thinking** to draw conclusions. This deliberate and reflective thought process helps determine what is true or false or right or wrong. While there isn't anything true or false or right or wrong about wearing socks to bed, we still use critical thinking to draw a conclusion about this opinion. In fact, we use critical thinking every day. We use it to pick out an outfit for school, for example. We also use it to consider important issues, such as if animal testing should be banned.

We've all seen the commercials showing abused and hungry animals as heartfelt music plays. These commercials certainly stir an emotion in us that wants to protect animals. And we should protect animals. No creature should be subjected to cruelty. So what does this mean in regard to animal testing? Is animal testing cruel?

In the United States alone, about 26 million animals are used to test and develop medical treatments to ensure safety for human use. Animal testing has been in use since ancient times. Those who **advocate** for animal testing believe this is the lesser of two evils. If we didn't test on animals, we'd have to test on humans. But those who oppose testing on animals believe that it is inhumane to experiment on animals. Animals and humans are also very different. The results of these experiments could be irrelevant and have no bearing on humans. What do you think? Read the pros and cons to this debate and decide for yourself!

Using animals in scientific research goes back to ancient times. Ancient Greek **philosopher** Aristotle and doctor Erasistratus are considered the first to have tested on animals.

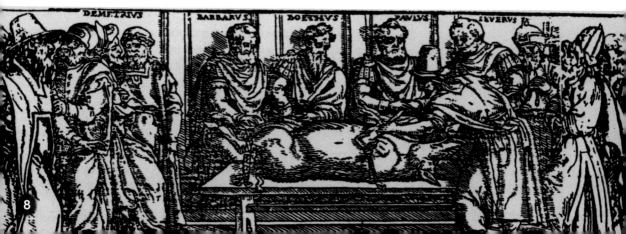

The issue of animal cruelty is often associated with animal testing. In the United States, more than 111 million rats and mice are used in animal testing a year.

Your position is strengthened when you can consider the opposing argument and provide reasons why you disagree with it.

MIDDLE GROUND VS. COMMON GROUND

Practicing finding the middle or common ground with others who disagree with us is important. Sometimes this is needed in order to keep the peace with our friends and family. While the two terms may sound the same, they're completely different. Finding the middle ground is used to resolve a conflict. Two parties who don't agree can find a compromise that they both agree on. While silly, a compromise for wearing or not wearing socks to bed would be to only wear one sock.

Finding common ground, however, creates and develops bonds with others. You and your friend's need for sleep is a common ground. Another common ground is liking funky-patterned socks. Of course, there will always be issues that people cannot compromise on. These topics require the most rational discourse, critical thinking, and empathy. What would be the middle and common ground for animal testing?

CHAPTER 1

Supporting Animal Testing

Why might someone support animal testing?

Since as early as the 3rd century, animals have been used for research. Famous Greek philosopher Aristotle and father of **physiology** Erasistratus both experimented on animals. We also have animal testing to thank for surgical procedures. In the 1100s, doctor Ibn Zuhr used animals to test certain surgeries before performing them on humans. Zuhr helped transform and advance medicine during the 11th century. Since then, animal research has come a long way. Back then, people had no guidelines on how to humanely treat animals during research. Today, we do.

Researchers agree that animals should be cared for before, during, and after testing. Animal care is important for a trustworthy and repeatable study.

COMMON FALLACIES

Logical **fallacies** are common errors in reasoning and can be persuasive. However, they invalidate or weaken an argument.

- *Hasty generalization:* This fallacy happens when a person assumes that all things are a certain way based on one example.

- *Red herrings:* This fallacy can also be considered a distraction or off-topic point. Red herrings are irrelevant information used in an argument, often to misdirect or confuse the other person.

- *Straw man:* Whether intentional or unintentional, this fallacy misrepresents the other person's argument. It often involves exaggeration, taking the argument out of context, or oversimplification.

Many studies that use animals in their research have veterinarians on their teams to care for the animals being tested.

Guidelines for Humane Animal Research

The U.S. Department of Agriculture has specific guidelines for the use of animals in labs to ensure that they are not mistreated or mishandled. These guidelines were adopted in 1966. Laws ensure that animals in labs have proper housing, socialization, food, and clean air. Animals must be given **anesthesia** when they undergo procedures that would be painful without it. Every research lab is required to create a committee that makes sure these laws are being obeyed. Researchers also have an incentive to treat animals well. If animals used for studying **immune** responses feel pain, it could hurt the study's results.

Medical Advancements

We have animals to thank for the advancement of medicine for humans. The vaccines that protect against deadly conditions like polio, typhus, diphtheria, whooping cough, smallpox, and tetanus were all created using animal testing. Countless human lives were saved because of animals. For instance, the world's first vaccine was created with the help of testing on cows. It helped end smallpox! We have the polio vaccine because of testing on monkeys, mice, and dogs.

Many vaccines and medicines would not have been developed without animal testing. According to British science academy the Royal Society, almost all modern medical breakthroughs are due to animal testing. Animal research and testing have helped advance medicine, from vaccines to organ transplants to mental health.

Animal research is used mainly to learn more about basic human biology. There is so much scientists don't know about the human body!

Scientists follow the "3 Rs" in animal research: replace, reduce, and refine. Scientists are encouraged to **replace** use of animals in research. If that's not possible, they're asked to **reduce** the number of animals used and **refine** how the animals are cared for.

According to the society, while computer simulations, **cell cultures**, and **epidemiological** studies are important, they are not enough to replace animal testing.

No Other Alternatives

Newly developed medicines are first tested on animals in order to ensure safety for humans. Skipping the animal testing phase is not normally an option. Vaccine regulations require researchers to prove that a new vaccine works and is effective on animals before testing on human volunteers. This avoids possible harm and unknown hazards to humans. However, an exception was made for the COVID-19 mRNA vaccine, as it was an emergency. There was a global outbreak of a new disease.

Animals are also the only other living organisms that are close to humans. In fact, some animals share almost a 100 percent genetic match to humans. For instance, a mouse's genetic profile is a 98 percent match to a human. Chimpanzees are a 99 percent match. Researchers use the similarities to determine how humans would react to a new medication.

BE DIPLOMATIC

The key to a successful argument, or debate, isn't winning and knowing all the facts. It's being diplomatic. This means being respectful and allowing the other person a chance to voice their thoughts without interrupting. Being diplomatic during a debate requires active listening.

Many makeup and other cosmetic companies test on animals. But they can't do this in the United Kingdom! This practice has been illegal since 1998. Many U.S. states also follow this practice.

CHAPTER 2

Opposing Animal Testing

Why might someone oppose animal testing?

People may have many reasons to support animal testing. But there are also countless reasons why people oppose animal testing. A few reasons include animal suffering, quality of life, and the negative consequences animal testing has on humans.

Animal Suffering and Quality of Life

The number one reason people are against animal testing is that animals suffer painful experiments when scientists use them in research. According to People for the Ethical

Many countries are looking for ways to eliminate animal testing. In 2021, South Korea introduced the world with its plan: the "2030 Chemical Safety and Animal Welfare vision."

Although animal testing can prevent harm to humans in some cases, it can cause harm to the animals being tested.

Animals that are deprived of social interactions with other animals can become aggressive.

Treatment of Animals (PETA), more than 100 million animals are killed in the United States a year for science experiments, product testing, and medical training. Despite having laws in place to regulate animal testing, inhumane practices are still being done to animals. Science has proven that animals think and feel, but they are still subject to abuse in the name of medical progress. For instance, animals have had holes drilled through their skulls and have had to inhale toxic fumes. Animals have had their skin burned, spinal cords cut or crushed, and been kept in restraints for hours. Animals used in testing are deprived of their natural habitats, food, and company of other animals.

Research shows that about 70 to 95 percent of animal testing can predict toxic effects in humans.

Animals Aren't Humans

Some animals may share an almost 100 percent genetic match to humans. However, that doesn't mean medications tested on animals will have the same effects in humans as they do in animals. In fact, bananas and humans share about a 50 percent genetic match—but no one is testing medicine on a banana! Genetic matches in different species may not produce valid results. Animals and humans are different. Scientists have been able to cure cancer and HIV/AIDS inside of mice for some time now, but these results can not be recreated in humans.

ANIMAL RIGHTS ACTIVISTS

There are many special interest groups that fight for animal rights. Cruelty Free International (CFI) is a UK-based organization that fights to ban using cats, dogs, and primates in animal testing. PETA is another organization that seeks to "expose animals suffering in laboratories, in the food industry, in the clothing trade, and in the entertainment industry."

There are many studies and research that suggest animal testing is unreliable. But there are just as many studies and research that claim the opposite.

Deadly Consequences

Animal research has led to gain-of-function research in **virology**. During gain-of-function research, scientists try to increase the deadliness or **virulence** of a disease by causing it to **mutate** inside an animal. In 2012, a group of scientists purposely engineered the bird flu virus. They wanted the virus to be transferred between ferrets. Some scientists believe that this type of research is necessary to understand how to best fight deadly diseases. They claim that gain-of-function research helps us be better prepared in the event of real-world mutations.

However, many people fear that a lab-mutated virus could be accidentally or purposely released. In fact, lab outbreaks have happened in the past. In 1972, a lab assistant working with live smallpox virus accidentally infected two people with the deadly virus. In 1976, the H1N1 virus was accidentally released from a lab. It caused at least one death, and at least 13 people were hospitalized.

There are many advantages and disadvantages to testing on animals. Many believe there's no other choice. Others say this isn't a good enough reason. What do you think?

DEBATE THE FACTS

During a debate, sometimes emotions or opinions can get in the way. Sometimes debates can go off topic. The important thing is to stay respectful and keep the debate on topic. If you feel yourself or the other person getting emotional, it's okay to take a step back.

Activity

What Do You Think?

You've read the pros and cons, or the affirmative and negative arguments, for animal testing. What are your thoughts? Use the critical thinking and debate tools you've learned to create an informed opinion and argument. Remember, you can always change your mind at a later time, especially when faced with new facts or viewpoints. A few things to consider while researching and debating topics like animal testing:

- What is my position on this?
- Why do I believe this is right or wrong?
- What evidence do I have to support my position?
- Is the evidence based on facts, feelings, or opinion?

Learn More

Books

Sepahban, Lois. *Animal Testing: Lifesaving Research vs. Animal Welfare.* North Mankato, MN: Capstone, 2015.

Terp, Gail. *The Debate About Animal Testing.* Lake Elmo, MN: Focus Readers, 2018.

Websites

Kiddle—Animal Testing Facts for Kids
https://kids.kiddle.co/Animal_testing

YouTube—Animal Rights vs. Animal Welfare: What's the Difference?
https://www.youtube.com/watch?v=Xa2OX6dEjwE

Glossary

advocate (AD-vuh-kayt) to support

anesthesia (aa-nuhs-THEE-zhuh) loss of sensation with or without loss of consciousness, used to block pain during medical procedures

cell cultures (SEL KUHL-chuhrs) process of cells being grown for research

critical thinking (KRIH-tuh-kuhl THING-king) carefully analyzing facts in order to form the best conclusion possible

empathy (EM-puh-thee) to relate to or understand another person's feelings or experiences

epidemiological (eh-puh-dee-mee-uh-LAH-jih-kuhl) relating to the study of how diseases spread and can be controlled

fallacies (FAH-luh-seez) incorrect beliefs based on arguments that are not logically sound

immune (ih-MYOON) highly resistant to disease

mutate (MYOO-tayt) to undergo a significant change

opposition (op-uh-ZISH-uhn) the state of disagreeing with or disapproving of

philosopher (fuh-LAH-suh-fuhr) person who seeks wisdom

physiology (fih-zee-AH-luh-jee) science that deals with living matter

rational discourse (RAH-shuh-nuhl DIH-skors) using reason or logic to think out and solve a problem

virology (vye-RAH-luh-jee) the study of viruses

virulence (VIHR-uh-luhns) a disease's ability to infect a host

Index